PROFOUND VERS-A-TALES

Order this book online at www.trafford.com/08-1408
or email orders@trafford.com

Most Trafford titles are also available at major online book retailers.

Note for Librarians: A cataloguing record for this book is available from Library and Archives Canada at www.collectionscanada.ca/amicus/index-e.html

ISBN: 978-1-4251-8902-0

We at Trafford believe that it is the responsibility of us all, as both individuals and corporations, to make choices that are environmentally and socially sound. You, in turn, are supporting this responsible conduct each time you purchase a Trafford book, or make use of our publishing services. To find out how you are helping, please visit www.trafford.com/responsiblepublishing.html

Our mission is to efficiently provide the world's finest, most comprehensive book publishing service, enabling every author to experience success. To find out how to publish your book, your way, and have it available worldwide, visit us online at www.trafford.com/10510

www.trafford.com

North America & international
toll-free: 1 888 232 4444 (USA & Canada)
phone: 250 383 6864 • fax: 250 383 6804
email: info@trafford.com

The United Kingdom & Europe
phone: +44 (0)1865 487 395 • local rate: 0845 230 9601
facsimile: +44 (0)1865 481 507 • email: info.uk@trafford.com

10 9 8 7 6 5 4 3 2 1

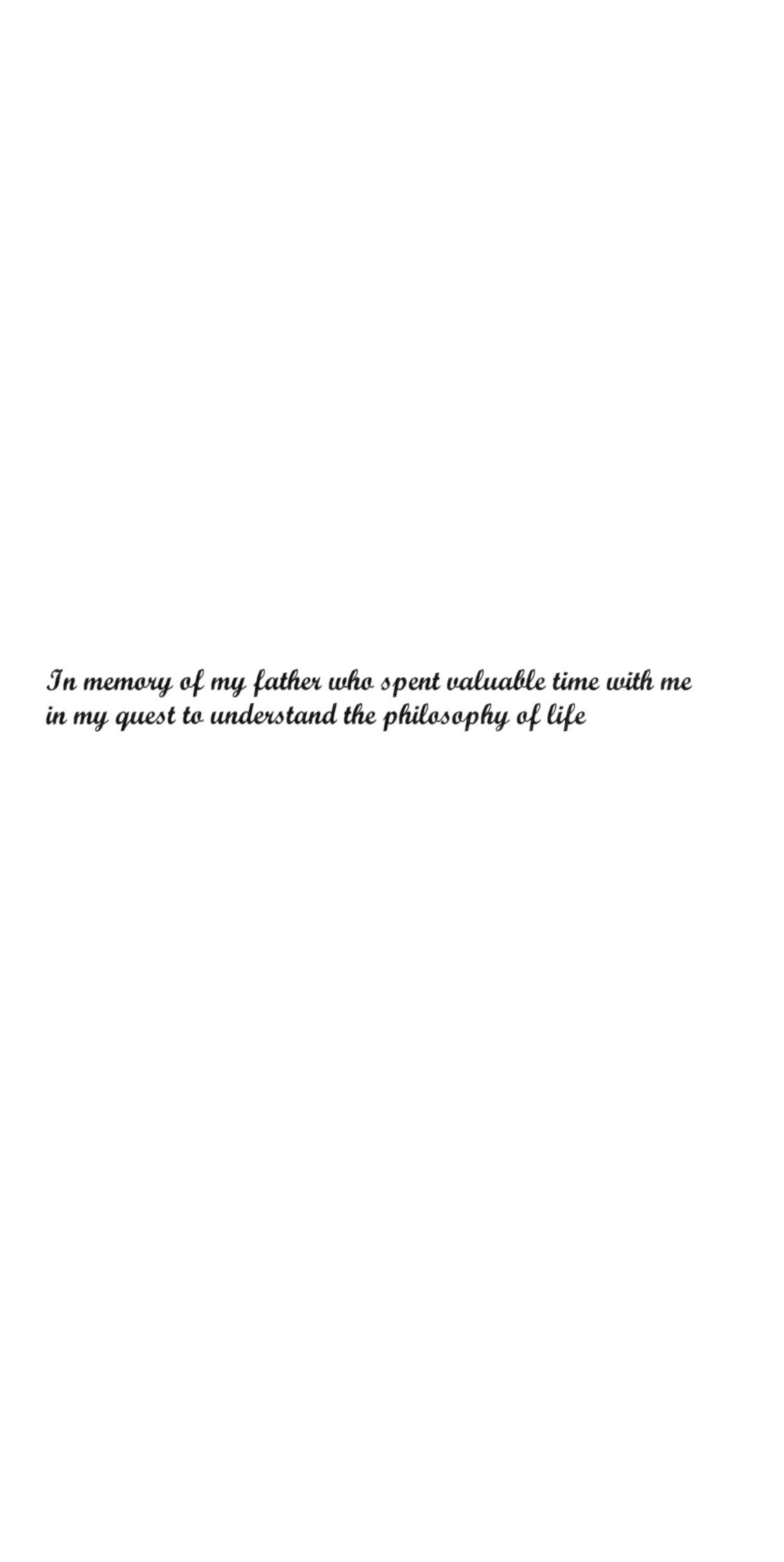

In memory of my father who spent valuable time with me in my quest to understand the philosophy of life

THE BEGGAR

She stands there all day, with her long stringy hair
Dirty and matted from days without care
Her long slender arms shakily extend
Long unkempt fingernails on fingers that won't bend

The few coins in her rusty cup rattle with each spasm
They only serve to widen the societal chasm
We stand and we stare, not daring to come close
We're ashamed of her clothing, her smell offends our nose

Guilt is the reason she does receive some alms
We look directly at her, she extends her palms
We drop a few loose coins, we rush right past
Don't really care if she'll be using it for repast

Is she below us, do we feel regret?
Could she be our future and we just don't know it yet?
Are we our children when they get to our age?
Are our children us, remember that stage?

Remember how you said to appear in control
"Don't worry my friends, I'll join the patrol"
And did you not rove and did you not roam
How about the longing to escape your home

Your daddy would sigh, your mommy would weep
You gave them emotional cuts that were deep
You left them with scars which they covered with love
Eventually they ask what you're thinking of

For in their eyes you're God's gift to them
We are not the tree, the leaf nor the stem
We are the fruit that attracts other clans
Outsiders will appear and make further plans

Your own life comes first, your parents aside
Your wife is now boss, let her decide
Your parents are not welcome your wife has declared
Her folks are important, they are revered

So slowly it turns, you see, that wheel of time
Forever it goes, it's very sublime
You have no real family; your wife's are your kin
You have no backbone; you just have your skin

For your spouse you see, had known all along
She will get her way as time marches on
In time you will kneel and beg her to stay
Two kids in hand she'll tell you "No way!"

You come to the point in life where it seems
Your power is gone and so are your dreams
Your clan that you thought was in your control
Somehow it seems you've lost your role

You are what God ordered, you just didn't know
Your parents had known, they told you so
You didn't believe them, they made no sense
Only in time would you recompense

You grovel and cry; your life's at an end
Your pals you deserted, you don't have a friend
Your mom and your dad are still on the fringe
You put them there yourself, you start to cringe

And what do you have to show for yourself
No money, no home, no food on the shelf
You look all around you, strangely in awe
"Now who do I blame for this faux pas?"

"My parents, of course, for whom else but they,"
"Came to my rescue when I went astray"
"They should have left me to fend on my own"
"My teenage years were set to my tone"

You feel that burning need to get in touch,
You realize now how you miss them so much
Ten years have passed since you last made contact
Things must surely have changed and that's a fact

You search the directory at their last known abode
Hoping to find them, not knowing what load
They carried for a decade while you were gone
The light in their hearts now no longer shone

Your daddy had died heartbroken and sad
A lingering illness that drove them both mad
The house they had sold along with their hope
The sickness would cost, they couldn't cope

A pauper's funeral, paid for by the state
A solitary mourner saddened by her fate
With nothing to live for and full of despair
The future for her looked dark and unclear

Her two closest kin; both men were now gone
No friends they had left; they had both withdrawn
No word from you, their sadness did show
Friends would tell them, "I told you so!"

Their friends had all noticed their doting on you
Their kind words of wisdom would certainly ring true
Your parents couldn't bear to take their advice
You were their only, their pride and their vice

And so it was clear when you did walk away
Forever they'd be in life's disarray
Not wanting to admit to their friends they were wrong
Those friends they had asked to move on along

And now you are seeking to find what you've lost
Ten years have passed you don't know the cost
Your mother is homeless, the number you called
No longer exists, no longer installed

For in her dementia she's out in the street
Begging for alms for something to eat
Forever in her heart she'll be on her quest
Looking for someone she loves the best

Her Alzheimer renders her capable she's told
Of remembering your face; things that are old
Yet she does not know where she slept last night
She does not recall once it's out of sight

And so she stands there sad and alone
The cold she can feel right to her bone
The Parkinson is causing her body to shake
Whatever they give her she's willing to take

Tomorrow will come and leave as today
One more troubled day of life's full array
Her heart is still burning with her love for you
Seeking to find you, the son she once knew

Tonight she will sleep all tortured and weak
Dreaming as she does every night of the week
Of the two men she loved, husband and son
While life's ancient debate keeps raging on

Does the love of a parent equal that of a child?
Does a child even care while running wild?
Doesn't life's poisoned darts slowly sap you of life?
Does realization appear like a double bladed knife?

So tomorrow will come and again she will sigh
One more day in her journey as time passes by
For that is the one thing that she hates the most
Time is against her; can't afford to coast

Tomorrow she'll stand on another crowded street
Waiting to see if her son she will meet
Each stranger she sees makes her heart skip a beat
But as they approach her, she's chilled with defeat

Her heart sinks again for the thousandth time
Her mind will not let her give up but climb
Life's torturous ladder; the one with no end
Her mind and her soul; through life they will wend

Resolved in her heart that elusive destination
Tomorrow she'll awake with renewed determination
That burning image of a son in distress
"Hold on my son you need my caress!"

That poor old woman, she senses your plight
She knows that you have lost your will to fight
Even in her madness she feels the true pain
Parents do feel when offspring complain

She knows that you need her; she's calling your name
People are laughing; they think it's a shame
"That crazy old woman," they would often deride
"Calling some name, all messed up inside!"

Tomorrow she will be a new city bound
Continuing to search until you are found
Unable to keep her place in this world
One day she'll see her dreams unfurled

But God only gives what you are able to endure
At the end of your suffering there's always a cure
For one day her torture will come to an end
She'll die a childless mother without any friend

Now look at yourself; look deep inside
Maybe the same fate awaits you outside
Your children, you know, are a part of you
Forever you'll search for your children too

And those of you men who are smarter than most
Think well of your parents; they will be that post
You are forced to lean on when life beats you down
Speak to them kindly; don't show them your frown

Your children will look up and follow your example
Whatever you dish out will be theirs to sample
You abandoned your parents; you've made a decision
To be cast away with surgical precision

So next time you pass some beggar on the street
Make sure you give her something to eat
Help feed her body to keep it abreast
With the strength of her soul in it's eternal quest

She may be the mother you forgot all about
The one you're now desperately trying to seek out
For etchings of time have carved on her face
Deep lines of worries; she looks out of place

Is she your mother or is she mine?
"Oh no," you will say, "My mother is fine."
So next time you make this false declaration
Remember that woman; she is your salvation

CHARITY

Charity begins within the heart; it speaks out loud and clear
A smile can sometimes serve to lift another from despair
Words and deeds in thoughtful ways; show someone true care
Respect for God's creative works; conform to laws we share

Accept the limits of the mind and make the most of time
Consistent thought with careful plan will captivate and prime
An audience that receives with trust starts from the core of self
Demanding all that must endure; let conscience be the elf

Forgive with zest and feel the joy when tensions dissipate
Do not delay to clear the soul of lingering thoughts of hate
Emotions that are aimed to harm will self implode and waste
Retention of a force divine; be wholesome, calm and chaste

Speak out at will with honest flow; let truth be light and guide
Select a passion for the thrust; compassioned sense of pride
Reward is gained by giving up possessions real and dear
The lifeline that is thrown with care; tenfold the blessed sphere

Listen hard for hidden pain and comfort when desired
Direct the anguished to the source as culpably required
Do not retain the urge to judge; perception's best is flawed
No perfect life has walked the earth; that image rests with God

The burden of a conscious wrong will render cause for strain
Correction of the errors made; true character regain
Dispel the fear of worthlessness; strive towards a high ideal
Deliver what was bargained for; stay honest in the deal

Alignment with a humble group will teach respect and awe
Compelled by good; the heart is filled; deception must withdraw
The donor of a compliment should not deceive for gain
When vanity becomes the norm let modesty remain

Self control and discipline are soldiers of the mind
Respect for self will guarantee a temperament refined
Display a sign of fortitude when faced with life's dark knights
Repel attack with shields of good carved from the guiding lights

The first real task is loyalty to mother who stayed true
Beyond the edge of certainty; devotion past the due
As parents should and always be; responsibly respond
To bloodline brought into the world; a mandatory bond

The germ of goodwill should start within the family value core
Then radiate through with rippling rings; reach out; full explore
Caress with cherished moods aglow; the seeds of love to sow
Allow the brilliance of the deeds to circle and then grow

Let laughter emanate from deep and spread like a disease
Contagious touch to bring relief and offer full release
Begin with love and end with trust; be cautious but be real
A special place in time and realm; existence is the seal

THE MIDNIGHT CAFE

Bring me another tea my friend and tell me once again
Pull up your chair a bit more close and tell me of my pain
You seem to know the ache inside; you said you felt it too
I'm curious now that you have said you'll tell me what to do

For you must know a magic spell; inside of me you've seen
How can you tell the way I feel and where my life has been?
You just seem to understand my life in every way
Your knowing nod; your gentle smile; you've left me in dismay

The tale you tell relates so well; it is my own life story
Your present's great; your future's bright but then your history
Puts you back in time my friend to where I am today
All broken up and hurt inside; can't seem to find my way

So how then can you say dear friend that you were once like me
You don't look sad; you always smile; your life is full of glee
And if you mock me friend of mine you have my guarantee
I'll seek whatever means I find to break from you and flee

For you have asked to sit with me; this café is all filled
My tea was cold I was about to go and get my mug refilled
You sat right down; noted my frown; sensed my life's despair
You stared at me; I looked away for fear that you might care

And then you asked as if by cue, "Something I can do?"
Avoided eye contact I did, and answered, "No, I'm through."
As I got up to walk away you turned to me and said
"May I please have your company; we'll share a piece of bread"

I stalled right there about to rise and pondered for a while
"No harm," I thought, "A crowded place; I could use a smile"
I sat back down and then I said, "Okay, if you insist."
You sprang right up and walked real fast; boy did you persist

You got in queue and waited there; a long line that's for sure
Your main objective, or so it seemed; give her lots of cure
And you returned two cups in hand; I could not comprehend
How come we've never met before and yet I call you friend

The bread you brought is sitting there all crumpled and uneaten
I pawed at it and broke it up; just like me it has been beaten
You stare at me with searching eyes; I cannot turn away
Our gazes locked; you look at me and let me have my say

My heart and soul come pouring out; my life is on display
I plead with you to make me stop; my mind is far away
I tell you of my torrid life; the reason I am here
A broken heart; some loneliness; add a pinch of fear

My very true love or so it seemed, was once the world to me
The pride and joy I felt inside; I begged the world to see
I could not understand right then their wish for the demise
A bond so deep with flawless seams; no need for compromise

I did not see what they had warned; too blinded by desire
Too young I was; I did not know what real life would require
My fantasies were real; I did not care; somehow we'd survive
I worked and prayed; a common goal toward which we'd strive

Little did I know back then I would be filled with rue
We had a team made up of one which worked like it was two
I did not know nor did I care; the love would soon win out
My lasting hope and loyalty would never be in doubt

His friends were there; all seemed nice that fateful night we met
I did not heed their warning signs; a move I'd soon regret
My friend and I were sitting there; each with a glass of wine
A Friday evening ritual; the dinner was just fine

The weekend here; with little care we laughed with one and all
A precursor to the commitment and then I'd take the fall
His handsome face his caring ways; my heart he had ensnared
We used that night; a launching pad to follow dreams we shared

I fell in love I must admit, almost at that first sight
With fluttering heart and mindless care, I reveled in delight
How wonderful it was to feel the pain of cupid's darts
Those poisoned little arrows that gladden lover's hearts

As time raced on I slowly sank to new depths in my mind
One year spent in solitude; my partner now unkind
Requesting space to breathe; he walked out one cold night
The shock was real; I lost my mind; pondered on my plight

Not knowing what my next move was, I cried myself to sleep
A prayer in my head that night, "Oh Lord, my soul please keep"
For on that night the spark in me just flickered and then died
The aching for his company never really did subside

When I regained the strength to move a new day had appeared
The sun was up; memories awoke; reality check I feared
The sleep I had was troubled with emotions that were deep
Yet it served to keep me from the edge so dark and steep

The days had turned to weeks and months of longing for a sign
Of his desire to come back home; to tell me he was mine
The wait in vain was all I had; it kept me sad but sane
I could not leave my comfort zone; disabled by the pain

I lost my job; I could not work; my focus was off line
My boss was kind; he let me stay; no work did he assign
Eventually I had to leave; my time with them was through
Recommended by my boss so kind, therapy would ensue

And even though I tried real hard, I could not but agree
The torment that invaded me would never set me free
My therapist had tried her best; she coaxed me all the way
I told her of my suicide note; the one I flushed away

My one true friend I'd sacrificed; he did not like her flaws
Told me she was no good for me; felt threatened by her cause
I started making excuses each time she tried to meet
Did not want hear her words; the warnings she'd repeat

Just like all the rest of them I carved her from my life
To please him was my one sole aim; could not stand the strife
My folks at home stopped calling me; that was by his request
No longer did I see his friends; I worked at his behest

Isolated from the outside world; he kept me on my own
I went to work and came back home; we were so all alone
Some days he'd go on business trips; said he'd be back next day
Invariably he'd call and say he would extend his stay

The gifts he brought delighted me; I could not help but smile
Those lonely nights I spent at home were truly worth the while
Sometimes he'd cut short his stay; he'd show up unannounced
My joy and thrill both uncontrolled; I ran to him and pounced

Not only did I hunger for his touch and warm embrace
I also knew that breaking up would cause me much disgrace
For in my haste I turned my back on those who loved me most
I spurned their care; I walked away; disappeared like a ghost

A year has come and gone since then and now I must admit
My foolish acts of arrogance destroyed my poise and wit
I venture not too far from home; my courage at an ebb
Caught up like a helpless fly in life's eternal web

The daily trips to this café; the extent of my realm
Left all alone; directionless; no one to take the helm
Crippled by emotional wounds; unable to be free
A ward of the state I was; ashamed I must agree

The distrust that is part of me will creep up and abide
Each time that a stranger asks to sit down by my side
You don't seem to understand you should not gain my trust
I don't know what's come over me but tell you all I must

The way you told me of your past so thoughtful and sincere
Gave me the urge to sit with you; our lives I could compare
Now I know I'm privy to a counterpart in kind
No longer do I feel alone; you have opened my mind

The comfort that I feel with you; a new world I have found
My friend I sense a bond with you if you just hang around
No longer do I feel the urge to run back home and hide
I just feel to sit right here and let our worlds collide

And even though I know we'll part; may never meet again
I wish that you will someday see your help was not in vain
For our souls are the tarnished ones; like all the others here
A café filled with dead lost hearts; each one a broken pair

The suicide note I left this time will certainly be found
The sleeping pills; an overdose; my body on the ground
I look around this café filled and sorrow surrounds me
So many souls in distress here, each longing to be free

Just like us they walked in life tormented and abused
Each one with a darkened fate; abandoned and confused
The symbolic bread and tea you brought; a pretense of our past
No more need for nourishment; our souls don't need repast

Suicide is not the way to cope when everything is lost
It traps us here; souls earthly bound; we have to pay the cost
A coward's flight from destiny; our plight remains unsolved
Look around and see the pain; not one will be resolved

And then we stop to think about the ones we left behind
The ones who loved us most of all will have no peace of mind
The hurt we have inflicted them; unfair that they must pay
The ultimate in sacrifice; a loved one gone away

And yet the ones who caused us pain are not aware we've passed
Their lives moved on; new loyalties; that's how the die is cast
The final act in life's short play has brought us here tonight
We crossed the point of no return; too late to wish things right

This café will forever hold the ghosts of self demised
Souls are trapped on midnight track; our time is now revised
No more we'll see light of day; just darkness all around
The deafening bells of midnight toll; a constant dreaded sound

This cavernous home for jaded souls is large and without end
It's built to hold as many fools whose lives did not extend
Once entered there we shuffle around; the entrance disappears
No exit sign is visible; dark shadows feed our fears

We have no place to run and hide; our bare souls are exposed
Thrust into our bewilderment; we will not be reposed
I wish now that I did not take my own life with my hand
The mandate of a midnight snack of torment and remand

THE RECIPE

Let all the goodness come to light in everything you start
Offer all that you can give; be cautious with your heart
Venture not where you can't see the future bright and clear
Experience hardships; part of life; suppress the urge to fear

Lasting thoughts of countenance; the profile understood
Accept the force of revelry and elevate the mood
Utmost care to have your fun but hurt no one in jest
Gather all the light moments; compile them for the fest
Heaven likes to know we care; light hearted by request

Look at all that you have done and give yourself reprieve
Increase your leisure by the year; recognize and retrieve
Venerate yourself before you seek to admire other styles
Emissions from the heart once kind will generate true smiles

THE RIVER

Oh precious River, you twist and you bend
Through tall hills and forests forever you'll wend
You start as a trickle at your place of birth
You ebb and you flow at your widest girth

You always keep moving, with swift undertow
You fall off the edge and cascade below
You burst at the bottom, you strike with a might
Your roar can be heard from your foam of bubbly white

And yet as you move along on your journey
Serene are your waters, no more cacophony
Downstream will find a quiet demeanor
Animals will gather; you are their convener

For life you have given to all living creatures
And that as you know is the best of your features
They come and they suckle; you nurture with care
They dive in your waters; you cleanse them all there

You glisten by day as you bask in the sun
You shimmer at night when the moon is on the run
Counting the stars your waters glow at night
Flicking little diamonds in their rippling delight

Mesmerized onlookers will fall in a trance
Hypnotized by love; there will be romance
Softly you whisper in each and every ear
You bring lovers closer; they feel sincere

The moon will excite; a real lovers' boon
Its lovely reflection will dance to your tune
Together in tandem you sway and create
A song of delirium; a potion so great

Those helpless devotees from far away places
Will come to your banks entwined in embraces
They'll be hopelessly locked in love's deep persuasion
Eventually they're lured; become part of creation

And let us not forget the denizens below
They too are caught up in the afterglow
Little shots of moonbeam will pierce at their hearts
Why can't they express love living in those parts?

For your bed will offer the perfect atmosphere
Giving them sensations all giddy and unclear
Your swirling current will cause bodies to gyrate
Clinging to each other; they'll never separate

And so the party goes on until the early dawn
You have fulfilled your mission; it's time to move on
The creatures all disperse; they slowly move away
With daylight comes the longing to come out and play

But first they must allow their bodies to relax
A nap is what is needed; it's what the body lacks
They will be back to swim and frolic in your waves
The ones below will hide and play in your conclaves

Another day appears; you can't afford to wait
There's work to be done; it's what rivers hate
Fighting pollution is first on your list of chores
You regurgitate it and waft it towards your shores

Your next task is pleasant; you head for farmers' fields
You have to irrigate them; maximize their yields
You stop along the way there; someone is in distress
A boat with broken engine; a problem to address

You turn and ask the wind to help you navigate
Bring the crippled vessel safely through the gate
And once on land the sailors stand and offer a salute
You've saved their lives so many times; this they won't refute

Seeking your advice, Mother Nature will kindly ask
She's thankful for your presence and how you multi-task
She wants to know if you can do the job that she requires
She needs somehow to start rain showers to put out forest fires

She was inclined to let them burn; contain themselves and dim
But then she suddenly realized those flames had grown too grim
Panicked creatures screamed in fear; they wanted her to know
They were devoid of home and land and had no place to go

Without a thought about yourself you offer them some hope
A crisis of this magnitude no one but you can cope
You ask the sun to lend a hand; he must co-operate
Turn up the heat; your waters must excess evaporate

Rapidly build rain clouds above; they must not be too high
Prepare the forces for the task; the battlefield is nigh
Again the wind, your trusted friend takes over as you wish
Wind knows drill; he's in the team; a goal to accomplish

Wind takes his canons to the spot; they must be positioned right
He let those bombs of water go; he knows he'll win this fight
A sense of joy Mother Nature sighs; she can't contain the pride
She feels for you and all you do; you're always by her side

So this completes another task; one of your many deeds
Respect you earned, deservedly so; you satisfy everyone's needs
Accomplishments are too numerous and everyone just knows
You won't accept any accolades; you don't turn up your nose

And when all is said and done, you've been there from the start
You've seen the world from infancy; you've seen it fall apart
The secrets that you hold today are older than the hills
You bear witness to man's great bane; you know of all his ills

Forever you will cast your spell on all those who you touch
In some way they'll want to say, "Thank you very much!"
As if to say it's part of life, you'll just move on and say
"Don't mention it, it was a joy, I must be on my way!"

THE SEVEN

We look across a crowded room; teenagers at first glance
Arrested states with nervous smiles give prelude to romance
Attraction strong we find a way to circumvent and meet
We dance into each other's heart; our world is now complete

We stand together locked in love; beginning life's pursuit
Emboldened by our need to taste the sweet compassioned fruit
The people who are gathered here will witness our desire
Our whispered dreams now real at last; our nuptial vows inspire

We walk together hand in hand; the first time we're allowed
Impassioned hearts; there is no doubt; feelings strong and proud
Alone we share each other's thoughts; our beings start to gel
The wholeness of a psyche sphere; in honeymoon awe we dwell

You stand beside me tall and strong; secure in you I feel
Cemented by unvaried trust and life's sincere ideal
The children now are part of us; they look to us for love
Fresh new branches of family tree; as parents we're above

We sit together holding hands; contented paths we walk
Absorbed in time with memories and seldom need to talk
A quiet life has taken place; companionship by choice
Requested role of self retreat; grand parents without voice

I lie alone awake in bed; the aching won't subside
Delusional thoughts to keep me sane and hold you by my side
I say a prayer for both of us; I cry with constant grief
The longing to depart this world; a widow's stress relief

Two souls together endlessly; eternal bliss attained
Endorsed with blessings carved in time for loyalty sustained
The afterglow will light the way; a guideline for the heirs
Traditions of a family trend; a blueprint through the years

THE MONSTER

The old man said he didn't care about the life he led
Hedonistic tendencies displayed a common thread
A hidden cross he had to bear; no one to share the cost
Somewhat skewed to other views; his life was done and lost

If only he had opened up a smidgeon of his ways
A common group not far away; support for castaways
Throughout his term he never knew the common discipline
Felt isolated in his stead; kept dark thoughts deep within

Don't we all feel captured by the pressures of the land
Which one of us is master of a life in true command
Connection to the world at large; your part will be refined
Each time that you request a change that's pleasing to the mind

Religion is a tool to use to captivate the mass
The system though most onerous has stayed without surpass
The guideline for a life ideal leaves questions and self doubt
Confuse the mind; a simple plot; de-worth to be devout

The old man is a parody of life's tormented state
Spiritual start enforced by weight; suppress the reprobate
No outlet for impious thoughts; a festering of urge
The evil half is bottled up; a psyche without purge

Events that stimulate the role; formative years inspire
Actions wrought with transgression to feed a dark desire
Excitement from the little deeds; a need to persevere
A nagging call to grow the taste; progressive and severe

Insensitive mind created by continuous vile replays
Render victims toys to play; captive power displays
Guiltless calm at time of pounce on prey without defense
The thrill of hunt overwhelmingly strong; animalistic and intense

The cunning of a wily scheme worked out to last detail
Keep probing forces far away along another trail
The façade of disarming traits an asset to deceive
Recognition for good citizen works; their accolades receive

Cause fear to blanket city blocks; sew distrust among the peers
Continued unabated lust; bring local law to tears
Deranged delight from media views; keep souvenirs on file
Their misinformed conjectures only serve to break a smile

The confidence created by the years of non detect
Resultant flaw a trap is set; a dragnet in effect
A cornered fiend with cagey eyes too weary to resist
Relief is strong; the tension gone; no reason to persist

Sit back and let attention surge; co-operate with all
Embellish truth with tinge of lies; exaggerate to enthrall
Exchange knowledge of the crimes for promised leniency
Give sordid details of the acts; lack common decency

The shock effect will serve to feed a frenzied news network
Sordid details of dastardly deeds drive victims' kin berserk
Avoid a trial; a guilty plea; no death row stress to test
A prison cell; abode for life; protected from the rest

A sociopath; the old man is emotionally ill equipped
Remorse is not available; reality has not been gripped
Four decades of confinement did not dampen his desire
Recurrent dreams of frothing blood; obsession fueled fire

Two score he was when captured; one score delivering death
A voyeuristic urge at ten; gave evil its first breath
Compelled beyond controlled restraints; unable to desist
The teenage boy; demonic traits; nightmares with wicked twist

The taunting from the other kids did drive him to the brink
Parental wrath with bible slaps; no respite for the fink
Despondency; depression filled; the child withdrew with age
Alienated by the difference felt; grew cold and filled with rage

The vengeance that the mortal feels; corrupted justice filled
A cauldron on continuous boil; concoction cooked and grilled
Ensuing years would tell the tale; the cannibal force within
The hearts ripped out; the mutile carves; the missing human skin

The monster now was at an end; his fragile frame was weak
He cried with pain for twenty years; was treated like a freak
Arthritic joints deformed with sting; unable to arise
The prison staff just scoffed at him; ignored his plaintive cries

Required by the department rules; death vigil full in place
Disruption to their daily chores; their hatred for that face
Old man closed his eyes and gasped; the heaving chest now still
A giant celebratory toast; his death resultant thrill

THE FARM

I sat one day alone at home not wanting to go out
Intentions for a quiet time; of this I had no doubt
A TV show was all I had; my novel I had read
Viewed all the channels aimlessly not caring what was said

And then as if by some command, my channel surfing ceased
Was riveted by a program that dealt with the deceased
They showed a child with golden hair who disappeared one day
No trace was left; no clue was found; not much was left to say

A community hit with senseless loss; a grief beyond repair
The daily searches; broken hearts; the feeling of despair
His parents were consoled by all; the church began a fund
The rumor wind began to blow; society hurt and stunned

Each parent felt compelled to seek protection for their own
All children played within the sights of adults that were known
The night would fall on empty streets; dead silence filled the air
Mystery lurked within the dark and fed on abject fear

The townsfolk had to move on with their lives and daily chores
Then time tiptoed in gentle steps; the healing slowed the sores
The parents of the fallen kid just packed up and moved on
They disappeared; not heard from since; forever they were gone

The house described; the neighborhood; familiar to my mind
A nagging tug of memories that trauma had confined
I felt the blood go to my feet; my body numb and cold
I realized I was witness to a horrible truth untold

Intuition made me think about the box that I had stored
I had no interest in its worth; on the closet shelf; just ignored
I sprang up then and made a dash; unsettled and aghast
I poured the contents on the bed; a clue I needed fast

I sifted through the old items not sure for what I sought
The tinkling of the memory bell; a fuzzy distant thought
My fingers touched the little book; the diary of events
My eyes locked on; a frozen state; recall in need of vents

I picked it up; opened the strap; my fingers damp and cold
Uncontrollably my body shook; a history to unfold
I fumbled with that log of life; anxiety at a peak
A picture fell on to the bed; I felt myself go weak

The photograph lay facing down; a game of hide and seek
Type of play my brother liked; he'd laugh but could not speak
Instinctively I called his name; his giggles came to ears
The isolation of my world now touched with sibling cares

I gazed upon the photo's back; recorded stamp and date
With magnet pull, my fingertips were drawn to brush with fate
The portrait of the little boy; my notion was confirmed
The replica I gazed upon; the likeness re-affirmed

The Reporter moved to a new case; another mysterious death
I sat deflated; proof in hands; completely out of breath
The images that filled my head; my body in cold sweat
The nauseous spew of dinner left my carpet stained and wet

My right hand held the portrait; my left still clutched the book
Compelled by cautious curious urge, I dared to take a look
Recorded facts in mother's hand; half journal soiled with wear
The other half in bold imprint; Mr. Reid's continued bare

I swiftly scanned the pages for a précis of our past
The five entangled characters; a historied text broadcast
The studio that I called my home began to swirl and sway
The mystery of my personal traits; my life in disarray

I forced myself to settle down; I needed time to think
I knew by then I had the key to unlock a missing link
The number flashing on the screen; my cue to call and tell
The memories of an evil deed; long buried; must dispel

The call I made did initiate prompt action from the cast
They came to me; an interview; they listened to my past
The fissure leaked and soon became a torrent in its flow
The memories broke the thin veiled dam erected by escrow

With full decorum all around, respectfully they probed
My mind enwrapped with anguish which they tacitly disrobed
We made a plan to meet again; I needed time alone
That manuscript would tell the tale; its details now were known

The little boy that they had shown; the blood connected veins
Our parent dead we had no place; no one could feel our pains
Our mother died; an overdose; a drug induced reprieve
From constant taunts; no end in sight; unable to achieve

Was thirteen when she ran away; could not cope at home
The pressures of both school and rules just sent her on the roam
She hitched her way; a far off place; her looks belied her age
Too young to work; starving child; streets would be her stage

The urchins that became her friends; imparted their advice
They taught her how to steal and fight and hooked her on a vice
Drugs they used to dull their plight; would come in costly ways
Young bodies used for deviant sex; a pimp collects and pays

An accidental child I was; she hid her secret well
At fourteen years she did not know the symptoms that could tell
Complained of stomach cramps one day; delivery most unkind
The ambulance ride; the hospital; adoption papers signed

At two years old I'd come to know a world of hostile trend
Was disciplined without a cause; felt fear from every end
The woman; my adoptive mom; the ruler of the nest
Her husband was a spineless man who dared not to protest

I quickly learned to be the child most suitable to her
Stayed well within expected norms; too frightened to demur
The man was kind; a gentle soul; he dared not show he cared
When left alone we laughed and played; a basic bond we shared

The fateful night the call came through; another child was born
My mother now at sixteen years; was desperate and forlorn
Seven months with child; no prayer left; no work did she obtain
A starving gem; the glitter gone; the perverts did abstain

The tunnel that she stared into was dark and without end
Her child-like mind was frightened by the size of her distend
She realized she'd lost one tot; she often thought of me
Felt certain that she did not want her second child to flee

Made up her mind to end it all; her life and baby's too
Decided on a daring plan; a drug overdose would do
The hospital staff worked furiously; a battle fought in vain
The mother child succumbed that day; her goal she did attain

Unable to revive her form; caesarian birth revealed
A drug infested baby boy; his fate in life was sealed
Dependency on crack cocaine; a child with special needs
The records showed a sibling child; adopted by the Reids

That very night the Reids were called; first option to receive
The brother of their two year old; family bonding to achieve
The diary found in mother's clutch was given to Mr. Reid
Her memoirs left to be perused; the world to scan and read

Mrs. Reid, our adopted mom was happy to accede
The caring for a child not whole; the State would feed her greed
A special kid; a means to plug financial holes that leaked
It would also mean a free supply; a drug from which she reeked

The constant cries; convulsive bouts; my brother was a pest
Deprived of lifeline drugs he lacked; his body couldn't rest
The government issued stock of coke was used up by the wife
The husband quelled by an angry spouse; avoided marital strife

The irony of the circumstance; a tragic circle closed
The very drug that calmed the child; in her abhorrence exposed
Her tolerance for the whining child grew lower every day
She desperately tried to keep him there; the basement; far away

The little boy that she did hate; was needed more than all
The daily hits that she required increased in size and call
She cleaned us up when workers came to review our detail
She taught me how to smile and play; a happy family tale

The annual government trip was good; she worked a master plan
Gave baby half his dose; he squirmed and writhed; looked wan
Increase in daily intake would relieve his body's stress
The social worker left in haste; the matter to address

Delighted that her ploy had worked; celebrated with a score
Rewarded Mr. Reid and me; she let us out the door
With baby in her care that day she gave him twice the dose
The little angel slept all day; gave her time to repose

The following week was blessed with bliss; no laughter in arrest
The air was light; relaxed delight; our hearts content; at rest
Complete in her deliverance of a role play we endured
She gloated with a smiling pride; the future was assured

Too good to last; we dared not hope to keep the status quo
The lady Reid relapsed with time; once more her rage did show
Foul mouth spewed repulsive words; worse now than before
Short tempered bursts of savage thrusts invaded our serene core

This prolonged; my brother two; another government review
The charade of an ideal clan again obscured the view
His needles all were up to date; she acted like she cared
No reason for concern they felt; our guardians' love we shared

Felt smug in her deceit again; released us from our strain
A celebration of triumph; she'd once again refrain
That little boy had failed to grow at normal pace and depth
At two years old he looked like one; was mentally inept

Inevitably the day arrived when she could take no more
His constant whine; contorted face; his seizures on the floor
Substance that was meant for him now half consumed by her
Painkillers with the white powder; her continuous need to whir

Deliverance for my brother came on angels' wings one night
God sent for him; a vacancy; seraphic torch to light
His soul surrendered quietly; went gladly on its way
Abandoned corpse; a twisted wreck; testimonial on display

The Reids were in a panic when they realized what occurred
A triple dose to calm the child; a decision quite absurd
An attempt to stifle screaming from a suffering child in pain
An irony; a tragedy; mother's wish she would sustain

For thirty months he had endured a life of torturous fare
The little boy would cry no more; the Reids were draped in fear
A daring plan was worked out when action replaced shock
The garden would become his bed; interred at midnight clock

At five years old I knew enough to pretend all was well
I carried on with charming grace though dread in me did dwell
Could not escape her piercing eyes; her shrieking voice was shrill
Made mental notes to stay alert; to please her required skill

Dependent on the drug supply; a bold new plot emerged
Would hide the fact that brother died; the evidence submerged
At this point she sat me down and threatened me with harm
Said if I only breathed a word I'd join him on the farm

The numbness that pervaded me brought darkness all around
My mind conjured sick images of my body underground
She did not have to say much more; my pact with her was sealed
The cost too great to break the deal; their secret I concealed

We carried on with careful tread; to neighbors less was said
I went to school; an escape; forced dark thoughts from my head
Deliberately stayed away from friends; could not erase the guilt
The truth was stowed in a compartment my mind by reflex built

The government worker made contact; meeting date was set
The call was made one month before the baby's third was met
Suppressing the desire to flee, the Reids would need a ploy
Diversion was the tool to use; deplete the town of joy

The park would be the place to use; unnoticed acts abound
A family out on evening walks; a stroller pushed around
She asked me to go up the hill then down the other side
Accompanied them; I didn't care; nonchalantly complied

The network of unending paths; the winding trails that curved
Wheeled baby tote bereft of child to a riverbank less observed
Flipped the carriage on its side; strewn contents caught the tide
The semi darkness of the dusk; corrupted deeds did hide

Made our way back to the house; alarm was timed and planned
Called police; tapped neighbors' doors; displayed self reprimand
Concocted tale of baby left in buggy while I played
Our yard was fenced; good neighborhood; no concerns of a raid

The citizens opined their thoughts; conjectures in good faith
Discussions built on emotional surf; imaginings of baby's wraith
Officials manned a command post; organized search arranged
The volunteers were cautioned; don't confront a mind deranged

A hundred calls received and checked; false sightings everywhere
Not for a lack of good intent; over zealousness bred from care
The hunt continued dauntlessly all night without a pause
The searchers never felt fatigued; each driven by the cause

And then at dawn the eye of hope; a breathless jogger's scream
A baby's blanket caught in reeds among the rocks downstream
A foot patrol in hearing range; at once upon the scene
An empty blanket brought to shore; no sign of baby seen

Attention turned toward upstream; a logical decision made
Recovery of the objects that were caught on the river's grade
A shallow course; slow moving tide; clear waters to its bed
Waders spanned the water's width; and focused straight ahead

The hollow churn of despair felt when baby's cart was found
Adjusted breaths; light steps on toes; an ear out for a sound
The dogs deployed; vicinity combed; his name in tandem called
Park visitors polled; a media blitz; no sightings were recalled

Bad news for the grieving Reids; withdrawn from public view
Continued search for eight more weeks; diminished rescue crew
The house was sold in record time; the purchaser filled with care
The family's need to move away; the trauma too severe

Financial lift from church and home; a new State for new life
A fresh dilemma on the rise; a mentally fatigued wife
She failed to cope without the drugs; her fragile mind derailed
No option left; enrollment swift; psychosis ward availed

The husband stayed the course norm; strain of spouse not there
Raised the boy with structured rules; each one defined and clear
A working mind; a tool to use; a brand new life defined
The past obscured by current acts and future goals assigned

Guilt with which he lived each day was cause to make amends
He noted that in mama's book; said we'd always be good friends
Each entry made at end of day; he started where she stopped
Torch of truth; flames concealed; held tight and never dropped

The message came to school one day when I was seventeen
A direct blow; an endless blight; another life's routine
The man I held in high esteem; the stave from full collapse
Pillar of a young boy's strength; stayed memory from relapse

I buried him that autumn day; the grey chill matched my mood
Felt anger, fear and loneliness; a troubling attitude
His friends consoled the lost young boy; all standing at the grave
His wife not there; still locked away; unable to behave

Decision made that very night; alone at home I cried
Transition made from boy to man when sullen tears had dried
I gave up school that instant when I knew I must survive
Unskilled work would fill long days; no social life to drive

A simple life is what I craved; no friends did I acquire
My jobs would fund most basic needs; not much did I require
The charities were grateful; his possessions clean and new
A banker's box I stowed away; safe keeping of a few

For twenty years it's been my home; reclusive by design
A constant for a mind at risk; a faltering of the spine
I made the call to bring them back; the reckoning was nigh
I evoked from them a promise to refuse to broadcast why

The transfer from complacency to active lead and guide
The focus of unwelcome light; a weakness of my pride
The sudden surge to discomfort; a selfless truth pursuit
Correctness of the twisted facts; my memories in recruit

The longest journey undertook; a flight to back in time
Emotions like a pendulum swung; dark moods and then sublime
Relief was felt from burden lift; the weight of guilt concealed
Affliction from amnesiac deeds; a mental mass congealed

Paralysis laid its hands on me when I beheld the house
The visions of the ghastly past; four decades; forced arouse
With wobbly knees I steered the group; supported at each arm
The target plot; the garden with a sign the read, "THE FARM"

They didn't have to dig too deep; discovery of his trace
The load of earth they lifted out; the sifting done with grace
The matching medical records were a proof beyond a doubt
Another sad conclusion to a mystery; the truth now out

I brought him back and buried him; their remains I've archived
They play below with giggling fun; the basement romp revived
A third spot is reserved for me; abutted to the two
I hasten to my destiny; I know what I must do

I'll exit gladly from this world; my loss must not be mourned
Fixated with their beckoning smiles; this life has been adjourned
A passage fraught with worrying; now to an end by choice
The blunder of my mother's life; entrapped with no rejoice

The Mrs. Reid will stay her course; the ordeal of impair
They say she searches all day long; her mind beyond repair
The three lives that she thought she owned; elusive conjectures
Prognosis for a lengthy haul; in life there'll be no cures

THE GIFT

You may not be the most beautiful rose in the garden
You may not even smell as good; I beg your pardon
My eyes and heart behold you, my one unique treasure
Plucked and delivered by his grace for my ultimate pleasure

I may not warrant a second glance or cause heart flutters
I may not be too smart; pardon my occasional stutters
But I know I'm endearing to you; as you always assure
Dedication and loyalty; my fortes for you to endure

The love abounds with uncontrolled, unbridled verve
Our hearts are locked together; it's what we deserve
The laughter that rings out; heavenly harps on display
Continuous mirth; a bouquet of sweet delirium each day

Cultivated with trust and unbiased requisites contributed
Interspersed with anguished thoughts that are unrefuted
Our unadulterated love is watered with his divine blessing
Our time spent with each other; emotionally caressing

The lingering shadow of sadness on my heart I feel
The knowledge of earthly limits; respectably surreal
Our kindred spirits, unable to abort our mission of ecstasy
Will transcend the mortal boundary toward hereafter fantasy

Though death will separate us; if for a brief moment in time
We both will feel each other's presence as we continue to climb
To the height of new passion; uninterrupted without bother
Awaiting our return to the cherished promised gift of each other

THE BALANCE

If all we had was mind and soul and nothing more possessed
Our life would be much simpler; contented; less obsessed
And yet we are destined to have a body which feels pain
A casket for our spirit trapped; our mortal ball and chain

Fixation we experience with all things that we lease
Shortsighted in our own belief that ownership will please
This, even though we realize our mold's not ours to keep
Discarded when we exit for rewards we'd like to reap

We grasp for all that we can keep; not caring about the rest
Our greed will often lead us to a fruitless, endless quest
The more that we accumulate, the further we will stray
From everything that's good and right; our virtues slip away

Supreme we feel; superior bound; material wealth we wield
Manipulative; unkind embrace to enhance total yield
The target that we seek to find; the vulnerable and the blind
Will be the ones to testify; our actions will be defined

Fear not if you feel the need to contemplate your fare
Correction of the spiral to the realm of deep despair
Your own approach to life and love depends on your avail
Supported by your will to find the empathy so frail

Man's endless lust for carnal sins will run the world amok
The humankind will chant and pray and pursue Satan's rock
Disguised as a cloak of good; intentions dark and sure
Pulpits serve to launch assaults on desperates and the poor

The leaders of both men and land will have a cross to bear
Deeds and thoughts locked in a stance for everyone to hear
Deep influence pervasiveness; reactions full amassed
Outnumbered by the multitude, the meek shall be surpassed

Let this not disdain you, though, from pleasures that you seek
Honest gain from true belief; will keep your joy at peak
The peace in thought; contented heart; nirvana guaranteed
Possessions there for you to use then give back and be freed

Attachment to material wrought encumber our free thought
A constant fear of loss of worth for value that we've bought
In pursuit of the grandiose; we neglect alms and aid
Life's balance checks; exact and just; obligatory debts be paid

We seek to find true happiness with false hopes and pretence
The single most important role; our deeds we will dispense
Misguided by societal thrust, often times we fail
To keep our promise to our lord; his wisdom we assail

May you all be pleased to know there's answer for your soul
Your conscience will abide in all that you have deemed your role
Forgiveness is the one bold trait; elusive to the lost
Instinctively we seek to find a way to curb our cost

No matter what unfolds today, or if your life is strewn
Across a vast expanse of shame; make sentiment your boon
Compassion serves to guide you through the forest of true creed
A simple task to find your heart; for others we must bleed

Prosperity without charity; foundation laid on sand
Slow moving tides of nature's law will crumble and disband
Conciliatory steps available, beginning with a smile
Kind thoughts and words; a gift behold, upliftment for a while

Redemption mode, open remorse, for offenses that we spewed
Enlighten our path ahead; our lease on life renewed
Partitions lined with ignorance no longer block our view
Realization that the world abides amidst the good so few

Ever so caressingly the kiss of death will taunt
Memories pry from deep within; they'll torture and they'll haunt
Grimaced smiles of angels dark; brooding shadows that appear
A collective sigh for distressed souls; no time for deed repair

Summon up the spark inside and let the goodness flow
Be grateful for the chance to let another person glow
Be truthful to yourself and then be cautious with your charm
Overindulgence in yourself can bring you undue harm

Incorporate within your plans the mandate of self worth
Perception of the world at large begins from time of birth
The pressures of both time and place will influence the mind
A positive force the universe; connect and be aligned

DICTATOR

Reach deep inside that mind of yours and tell me what you find
Perhaps lots of unused space; still vacant; not defined
You claim to be the smartest of the clan of fools you lead
They worship you with fearful awe, from distrust that you breed

Call up your wit when you can sense your power start to fray
Surround yourself with enforcers; lay siege to rule the day
Swiftly strike the dissidents; eliminate the threat
Be cognizant of public views; hold court to subdue fret

Blame it all on someone else; the hardship that you cause
Respect for none; propaganda bound; demand loud applause
The evil that erodes your soul just festers and expounds
False virtues you have sold to them; sheer ignorance abounds

Define your goals with impunity; you're master of your turf
Command at will with no regard for the titled and their serf
The heavy hand of despot reigns with terror struck in hearts
Not one will have the courage to rise up and seek restarts

Captivated by your lust for power; addicted to your scheme
Enraptured with yourself; you push your ego to extreme
You let them starve; your break their will; no energy to fight
Few try to flee; are slaughtered there; near freedom in their sight

Suffocated thought; intellect reduced; unstable and unsure
A populace brought to its knees; deprivation to endure
Your presence felt in every wall; they whisper when they speak
You commandeered their kin to tell; family secrets they will leak

Create fear with military might; raid family homes at night
Secure your hold; increase your forces; sustain heightened fright
Smile and salute the world at large; convince them of great love
Use media as your tool in trade; declare yourself a dove

Reward yourself with luxuries and justify their use
In contrast to the citizens, their funds for your abuse
Declare yourself leader for life; with referendums that are fake
Unilateral governance rules apply; lieutenants on the take

Committed to your evil plot, your heart grows dark and cold
No longer can you see your sins; your evil deeds now bold
Your wanton lust for power has secured your place in hell
You will reside among the damned; torment has cast its spell

THE SYSTEM

Aspiring to a higher goal; obsessive drive to dream
The world that we experience will never be supreme
The limit of capacity; acceptance of the goal
The wisdom flayed; no favorites; attempts to save the soul

Correctness of the attitude; first order of the trait
Respondent fleets; subservient; we offer hope and wait
Directionless without a cause; the church is used to find
The motionless; unused resource; a mind to be defined

The final act is forced upon pariahs in review
Not one of us is pure enough; the mortal faults construe
Consider the emolument; less friction of the force
Embedded on the log of life; our deeds without resource

The standard set; a rule declared; the moral aftermath
Accept the norm; mediocre thoughts; a simple grasp of math
Surrender to the pressures of the structures built with time
Unquestioning faith with true belief; support or fail to climb

The balance of a deed of grant; the merit not confirmed
The hope sustained; resultant flaw; no bonus reaffirmed
The guilt is set; the level known; the sect of just rewards
The stern enhanced; most recent call; the changing of the guards

The system used; control the mass; effective use of claim
Direct the darts; individually aimed; expose the acts of shame
Forgiveness is the touted taunt; yet fear of wrath persists
Confusion is the strength of law; embodied cloak and fists

www.ingramcontent.com/pod-product-compliance
Ingram Content Group UK Ltd.
Pitfield, Milton Keynes, MK11 3LW, UK
UKHW020136250726
13967UKWH00002B/693

9 781425 189020